CULTURAL GENOCIDE

Thirteen Things You Haven't Been Told About Residential Schools, Mass Graves and Broken Treaties in Canada

DREW ELDRIDGE

Copyright © 2022 by Drew Eldridge

All rights reserved.

The cover image is a photograph of Kamloops Residential School, circa 1930. It's from Archives Deschatelets-NDC, Richelieu and is in the public domain.

Email: dreweldridge@protonmail.com

ISBN 978-1-7781088-7-7

NOTE ON THE TEXT

The following article was originally published in the Letter to the Editor section of Christian Voices in July of 2021 after the attacks on several Canadian churches. Thank you to everyone who reached out and encouraged me to have it printed into a booklet. I'm glad you found value in it and agree that the information contained is worth sharing with a wider audience. Anything to help stop the violence. If you are reading this for the first time or are wondering what attacks on churches I am referring to, here are a few headlines from 2021 that might help provide some context:

"Remains of 215 Children Found Buried at Former B.C. Residential School, First Nation Says"
   - *CBC News*

"23 Canadian Churches and Counting Under Attack"
   - *Western Standard*

"This Canada Day, Let's Remember: This Country was Built on Genocide"
   - *The Guardian*

"Two More Churches Burned Down in B.C's Interior"
   - *CBC News*

"Fifth Church Fire in B.C."
   - *CTV News*

"Two More Catholic Churches Burnt in Canada; Probably Linked to the Discovery of Mass Graves of Indigenous Children"
   - *Merco Press*

"More Churches Burned in Canada After Latest Grave Discovery at Residential School"
   - *Vice News*

"Statues of Queen Victoria, Queen Elizabeth Toppled in Canada"
   - *Reuters*

"At Least 45 Christian Churches Set on Fire in Canada as Attacks Escalate"
   - *CBN News*

"NDP seeking MPs' Unanimous Consent to Label Residential School Experience as Genocide"
  - CBC

"Burn it All Down': Head of B.C. Civil Liberties Group Resigns Over Tweet About Church Fires"
  - National Post

"Cultural Genocide: On Discovery of Hundreds of Graves in Canada"
  - The Hindu

"Ten Churches Vandalized with Paint"
  - Winnipeg Free Press

"Residential Schools Were Part of Genocide Plan, Manitoba's Indigenous Reconciliation Minister Says"
  - CBC

"The Burning of Canada's Churches"
  - Wall Street Journal

"A Map of the 68 Churches That Have Been Vandalized or Burned Since the Residential Schools Announcement"
  - TNC News

"Here's How Some in Northwestern Ontario are Reflecting on Treaties Recognition Week"
  - CBC

"Churches Burned Down as Anger Over 'Cultural Genocide' of Indigenous Children Sweeps Canada"
  - The Telegraph

"Churches Are Being Burned to the Ground in Canada"
  - *Loudwire*

"Residential Schools Were a Key Tool in America's Long History of Native Genocide"
  - *Washington Post*

"Churches Burned to the Ground in Canada in 'Anti-Church Hate Crime Wave"
  - *Fox News*

"Winnipeg Mayor Pledges to Support Bishop Grandin Renaming at City Council"
  - *CBC*

"Statue of the Queen Toppled as Canadians Protest the Mass Graves of Indigenous Children"
  - *The Daily Beast*

"'Terrible and Tragic': Century-old Catholic Church in Morinville Destroyed by Fire"
  - *CBC*

"Canada Pledges $40 Billion in Talks Over Rampant Abuses of Indigenous Children"
  - *NPR*

"Justin Trudeau Says Pope Francis Needs to Apologize"
  - *Huffington Post*

"Ontario Announces School Curriculum Changes to Mandate Indigenous Learning in Grades 1 to 3"
  - *CTV News*

LETTER TO THE EDITOR

2021

Hi Drew!

I'd like to ask you about the residential schools, the bodies discovered and the recent violent reactions to it. Did Christians commit cultural genocide? What is your opinion on all of this?

Susan T.
    Winnipeg, Manitoba

RESPONSE

IN DEFENSE OF OUR CHURCHES

THIRTEEN THINGS YOU HAVEN'T BEEN TOLD ABOUT RESIDENTIAL SCHOOLS, MASS GRAVES AND TREATY VIOLATIONS IN CANADA

BY DREW ELDRIDGE

That's an excellent question, Susan. Thank you for writing in! Yes, it's certainly true that cultural genocide is a common charge made against Christians in Canada. The popular narrative we're told is that European Christians came to North America, stole the land from the Indigenous peoples, wiped out many of their communities and then imposed things like residential schools on the survivors as a kind of assimilative "cultural genocide." Children were torn from their parents' arms and dragged to schools where, if they survived being systematically starved, raped or murdered, were forced to abandon their native spirituality and convert to Christianity. We are told that we should experience a personal sense of shame and guilt about this and take appropriate action. As the beneficiaries of that past, we should make amends for cultural genocide with regular public apologies, declarations of land recognition, demonstrations of solidarity, and advocacy of extensive material reparations. These accusations fuel resentment that can lead to the kinds of hate crimes against Christians that you've pointed out. But is it really true?

Well, I think the answer to that question is complicated, and I'm not sure I am interested in putting forth and defending a competing narrative at this point. But what I will do, since you asked, is lay out a list of facts that I've discovered, with links to sources that might help you figure out the answer for yourself.

I believe that much of the confusion that you and other Christians are feeling about this matter is due to many things that have been either ignored, forgotten or altogether omitted from public discourse. There are some things that many people are simply unaware of that make this narrative seem plausible, and which has unfortunately led to violence.

As surprising and disturbing as some of these facts may be, I hope people you share them with will understand their purpose is to help bring more truth to "truth and reconciliation." They are not intended to be provocative, but merely heard, reflected upon and digested. Nor are they meant to downplay anyone's experience of abuse or defend residential schools in any way. They should always be presented in our conversations gently and respectfully, in a spirit of love.

I will begin with a fact about colonialism and the myth about the state of affairs that European Christians supposedly robbed the native population of, and that we are often told they are now missing out on because of us. This is the first misconception that needs to be addressed. It's what's beneath most of the rhetoric about guilt and what grounds the narrative about cultural genocide as a whole.

IN DEFENSE OF OUR CHURCHES

Fact #1: The Indigenous people of North America regularly engaged in mass killing, mass burial into unmarked graves, theft, land seizure, rape, gang rape, torture, slavery, kidnapping, child abuse, religious indoctrination and breaking of land agreements for centuries prior to European contact.

The popular narrative begins with the notion that indigenous people were more or less living in harmony, sharing the land and enjoying an abuse-free, genocide-free existence until white Christian Europeans arrived and spoiled it. Tragically, however, everything from scientific archeological evidence to the journals of explorers confirms that, like everywhere else in the world, precolonial North America was a mixed bag of good people and bad people—with most being somewhere in between. There are a lot of great books that document all of this, if you're interested.[1]

In the journals, explorers praised and complimented many Indigenous tribes, especially for their kindness, generosity, bravery and sense of justice. Often, they would remark how the virtues displayed by some Indigenous people often put the average European Christian to shame. However, these explorers also documented how there were other Indigenous tribes in North America who were very different, and who often bullied and preyed upon the gentler, less warlike ones. Slaughter and burial into mass unmarked graves was one of these common practices.[2]

CULTURAL GENOCIDE

It might even be the case that graves found around residential schools have nothing to do with Christians and were there long before the schools were even built. Archeologists have methods of determining these things. Genocidal blood feuds were common as well, just as they have been in many other parts of the world. The Battle of Crow

Creek is one of the most heartbreaking examples. Archeologists have dated it to the fourteenth century.[3]

There is a little-known place called "Skull Tower." Many believed it was myth. The mass unmarked grave was discovered by archeologists in 2015.[4]

Explorers witnessed something called "The Scalping Dance" that some indigenous tribes performed after slaughtering rivals.[5]

After the men were ritually mutilated, women and children were taken as sex slaves. But even in many of the more humane tribes, explorers noticed that women and children were often treated poorly. Here is just one account by the explorer Alexander Mackenzie. Keep in mind that he writes this after praising these Indigenous people for other things.

> "... The females of this nation are in the same subordinate state with those of all other savage tribes ... The infidelity of a wife is punished by the husband with the loss of her hair, nose and perhaps life; such severity proceeds from its having been practiced without his permission: for a temporary interchange of wives is not uncommon: and the offer of their persons is considered as a necessary part of hospitality due to strangers ... the life of these women is an uninterrupted succession of toil and pain ... they are sometimes known to destroy their female children, to save them from the miseries which they themselves have suffered ... Many and various are the motives which induce a savage to war. To prove his course, or to revenge the death

of his relations, or some of his tribe, by the massacre of an enemy..."

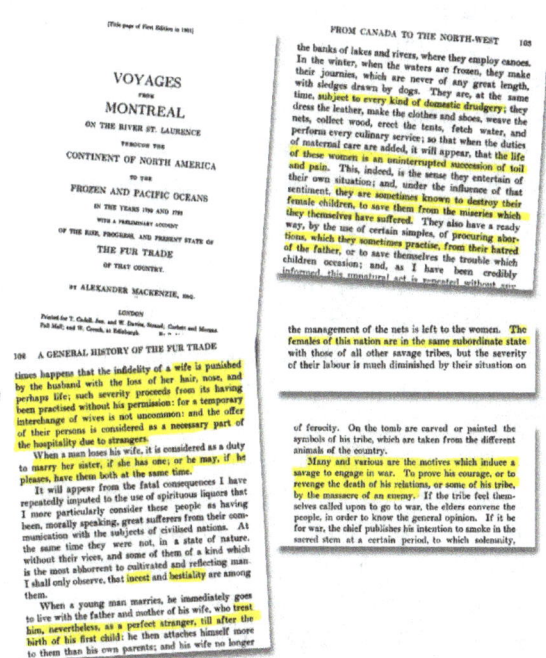

In other words, it is entirely a myth that Indigenous people were living in peace and harmony prior to contact with European Christians. One effect of this idea is that when unmarked graves are found near residential schools, they are called "evidence of a genocide." But when they are found anywhere else they are merely called "Indigenous burial grounds." This difference in judgement reveals the assumptions we make about what happened in these places.

Another documented traditional Indigenous custom was invasion and dispossession. Again, there are many books that reveal this.[6] It may be the case that indigenous tribes like the Sioux were wrongfully displaced through colonization. But the Sioux took the same land from the Cheyenne, who got it from someone else. The idea that this land was shared peacefully is entirely fabricated. Conquest was not something introduced by the European Christians. This brings me to the next myth.

Amidst demands for the Pope to apologize, you may be led to believe that the Catholic Church supported or encouraged the European displacement of Indigenous people. But is this really true? Here is Pope Paul III in his own words, writing in 1537:

> "The enemy of the human race, who opposes all good deeds in order to bring men to destruction, beholding and envying this, invented a means never before heard of, by which he might hinder the preaching of God's word of Salvation to the people: he inspired his satellites who, to please him, have not hesitated to publish abroad that the Indians of the West and the South, and other people of whom We have recent knowledge should be treated as dumb brutes created for our service, pretending that they are incapable of receiving the Catholic Faith.
>
> We, who, though unworthy, exercise on earth the power of our Lord and seek with all our might to bring those sheep of His flock who are outside into the fold committed to our charge, consider, however, that the Indians are truly men and that they are not only capable of understanding the

Catholic Faith but, according to our information, they desire exceedingly to receive it. Desiring to provide ample remedy for these evils, We define and declare by these Our letters, or by any translation thereof signed by any notary public and sealed with the seal of any ecclesiastical dignitary, to which the same credit shall be given as to the originals, that, notwithstanding whatever may have been or may be said to the contrary, the said Indians and all other people who may later be discovered by Christians, are by no means to be deprived of their liberty or the possession of their property, even though they be outside the faith of Jesus Christ; and that they may and should, freely and legitimately, enjoy their liberty and the possession of their property; nor should they be in any way enslaved; should the contrary happen, it shall be null and have no effect." -*Sublimis Deus, 1537*

This is an echo of the same thing Pope Eugene IV declared sixty years earlier, long before Europeans came to North America. He had been observing abuses in the Canary Islands and decided to make it perfectly clear what he thought the appropriate action of every true Christian should be:

"They have deprived the natives of their property or turned it to their own use, and have subjected some of the inhabitants of said islands to perpetual slavery, sold them to other persons and committed other various illicit and evil deeds against them. . . Therefore We. . . exhort, through the sprinkling of the Blood of Jesus Christ shed for their sins, one and all, temporal princes, lords, captains, armed men, barons, soldiers, nobles, communities and all others of every kind among the Christian faithful of whatever state, grade or condition, that they themselves desist from the aforementioned deeds, cause those subject to them to desist from them, and restrain them rigorously. And no less do We order and command all and each of the faithful of each sex that, within the space of fifteen days of the publication of these letters in the place where they live, that they restore to their pristine liberty all and each person of either sex who were once residents of said Canary Islands. . . who have been made subject to slavery. These people are to be totally and perpetually free and are to be let go without the exaction or reception of any money." [7]

Far from supporting things like slavery, displacement or subjugation, the Catholic Church was strongly and vocally against it, often threatening to excommunicate people who were involved. This is partly why the Indigenous people of Canada so often abandoned their older spiritual traditions. They saw the goodness of Jesus and the appeal of Christian morality. This brings me to the next matter— the myth of forced conversion.

Fact #2: Prior to the formation of Canada, Christian missionaries were generally welcomed by Indigenous people. Mass conversion was common and entirely voluntary.

I've mentioned the journals of explorers. But there are also reports of missionaries written over the centuries. Far from going place to place imposing Christianity on people, they typically went completely unarmed. The Indigenous people of Canada were often known for their curiosity about the creator and open mindedness about other religions.[8] The teachings of Christianity sometimes weren't even that different from their own. Many discovered and welcomed the idea that Christianity was a completion of, not a replacement for, their traditional religions. Today, many Indigenous people have chosen to continue embracing Christianity. Being a Christian doesn't mean having to let go of all Indigenous traditions.

Fact #3: From the beginning of the formation of Canada, the Canadian government offered full equality to the Indigenous peoples. Some accepted and some rejected the offer. The infamous Indian Act was the result of that rejection.

"Indian" didn't necessarily mean "an Indigenous person" in the 1800's. It was a word used to describe Indigenous people who didn't want to be treated as free and equally under the law. There is a commonly held belief that the Indian Act was created because Europeans were racist and wanted to treat Indigenous people differently. Nothing could be further from the truth. All of the evidence we have shows that the colonies believed Indigenous people had the full potential to live peacefully and productively as equals to them under a common law. The Indian Act was established in spite of, not because of, what most of them believed about Indigenous people. Some Indigenous people accepted the invitation. Others did not. For that reason, the Indian Act was established.[9]

Full enfranchisement was offered until 1985, when it was abolished. Today there is no path to enfranchisement—making Indians, in a sense, a permanently disenfranchised group.

Fact #4: Treaties were violated by both sides. Violations of the Canadian government were often in response to perceived violations made by others first.

If you make a deal with someone and they don't follow through on their side, then the deal might become null and void. Sometimes violations of treaties have been due to deception and betrayal. Someone might sign a treaty, but really have other plans. Other times, treaties are broken because members of the represented group don't feel like they actually consented to it. Not every Indigenous person who was affected by the treaties felt like Indigenous leaders of the day legitimately represented them. Consequently, treaties didn't always play out the way leaders on both sides expected or hoped.

On some occasions, violations were simply due to misunderstanding and confusion. Traditional Indigenous cultures and languages were often very different. And just because a few people at the top might have understood what was being negotiated or what exactly the implications were, that didn't mean that people on the ground always did. News traveled slowly back then. People interpreted things differently. It simply wasn't the case that everyone was on the same page when treaties were made.

Often, this resulted in people violating treaties without even knowing it. Nevertheless, these kinds of violations affected the validity of the deals made by the people who made them. Accident or not, a deal was a deal. This is why we believe it's fair to return and not pay for our food in a restaurant when they make mistakes with our orders. It happened back then with treaties as well, and it wasn't only one side making mistakes or being irresponsible. The debates about who broke what can be found in the primary sources. It's not always clear who was right, who was being most honest or who had the best intentions.

One example would be Treaty 1, which applied here in Manitoba.[10] A part of the agreement was the forbidding of alcohol to Indigenous people on the lands. The treaty reads that "the undersigned Chiefs do hereby bind and pledge themselves and their people strictly to observe this treaty. . ." Was this strictly observed? The treaty was also conditional upon them to "not interfere with the property or in any way molest the persons of Her Majesty's white or other subjects." Was this always observed? It's also important to remember that these post confederate treaties were signed under the pretense of gradual assimilation. This is what the Queen and newly formed Canadian government told them they were signing up for. It's why they agreed to fund things like schools. However, this means that any resistance to gradual assimilation would have been perceived as violations.

What I am saying is that no matter what you choose to believe about these things, it isn't as simple as "Canada violated treaties." Often in these situations, promises were broken because it was believed that the other side had broken theirs first.

Fact #5: The first residential schools in Canada were voluntary, welcomed and even requested by Indigenous parents and leaders.

The first residential schools in Canada were optional. Indigenous children didn't have to go unless their parents made them. Even the Truth and Reconciliation Report confirms this.[11] In chapter thirty, the section on parental resistance, it says the main ways some parents resisted was to "refuse to enroll students, refuse to return runaways, or refuse to return students at the end of summer holidays." The keyword here is "enroll." The examples given of resistance make it even more evident that these institutions were voluntary and refusals were possible.

In 1904, some Indigenous parents are on record for removing their daughter from a residential school. The response and argument of the principal, according to the Truth and Reconciliation Report, was in pointing out that the parents had "signed the admission form giving the government the right to determine when their daughter would be discharged." The parents left with the child. The principal warned them that there might be legal consequences. But the key thing to notice here is that they had signed them up. Parents, and even disappointed parents, were signing their children up for Christian residential schools.

But what about children being torn from their parents back in those days? Doesn't the Truth and Reconciliation Report address that? It certainly does. But it's worth taking a closer look at the language. Take, for instance, the section called "Separating Children from Parents." The very title sounds menacing. It makes it sound like the government was going in and dragging the children away. However, if you read closely, you will find that the word "separating" isn't actually referring to "forced removal." It's used in the geometrical sense of creating distance. Specifically, it is referring to a trend of preference among educators for long distance learning. The section could have just as easily been entitled "The Growing Trend Amongst Educators in Favor of Optional Long Distance Boarding Schools for Indigenous People."

The Truth and Reconciliation Report goes on to cite how Bishop Grandin wrote a letter to the Indian commissioner to "help him stop parents from taking their children" out of schools like Lac La Biche. But when you look at the actual letter of the bishop himself, what you'll find is that he was asking the commissioner to try and persuade parents, not force them. This was the nature of parental resistance and school counter resistance when there was any. But the important thing to take away from this is that they were enrolling and unenrolling their children.

Fact #6: It's true John A. MacDonald called for assimilation of Indigenous people. But it's also true that many Indigenous people did too. At the time, the vast majority of Indigenous people were Christian and wanted Christianization.

We have all heard the quote of Sir John A. MacDonald endorsing assimilation. But it's important to remember that assimilation wasn't really considered a bad word at the time. It wasn't something most Indigenous people found insulting—especially Indigenous Christians. For all assimilation really meant was the plan to aim for a society where white people and Indigenous people could live side by side as equals under the rule of law. "The great aim of our legislation has been to do away with the tribal system and assimilate the Indian people in all respects with the other inhabitants of the Dominion as speedily as they are fit to change." [11] In this respect, Sir John A. MacDonald wasn't all that different from Martin Luther King Jr. Education was considered one of the means to that end, just as it is today in all public schools.

Interestingly, the truly controversial position for a white person to have was that Indigenous people should be left alone. Many Indigenous communities lived in extreme poverty. Sovereign communities developed very serious problems, such as alcoholism and disease.[12] They also had difficulty competing on the global market. It was something they weren't used to doing independently. Worst of all, this often became cyclical. Education was considered to be a way of breaking the cycle and empowering these communities.

Sir John A. MacDonald is often accused of white supremacy. But wouldn't a true white supremacist be against integrating non-white people into their society? Think of all the money and time put into it. Today, Sir John A. MacDonald might be called a white supremacist and perpetrator of cultural genocide for his endorsement of assimilation. But back then he would have been called these things if he we were against assimilation. Poverty and disease in isolated Indigenous communities was sometimes so rampant that non-interventionists would be accused of letting the Indigenous people go extinct.[13]

Fact #7: The increase of residential schools was caused by the increasing demand for them by Indigenous parents and pressure put on the government by Indigenous leaders.

While it may be the case that these optional residential schools had a slow start, they soon became so popular amongst Indigenous parents that the schools were often over crowded. Complaints about over-crowding and under funding put pressure on the government to provide more. In economics, there is something called the law of supply and demand. In the case of residential schools, the government and churches provided the supply and the parents provided the demand. Here are examples of such petitions. Notice that these are all-Indigenous unions. Notice that they are asking for more and better schools that will help prepare their children for "civilized life." You can easily find them by using the achieve search engine.[14]

"We would prefer to see our children without instruction rather than have their education taken out of the hands of Priests and Sisters, who for more than half a century have been sharing all our adversities and were often the sole protectors of our rights." -Fort Vermillion Reserve, 1946 (https://parl.canadiana.ca/view/oop.com_SOCHOC_2003_2_1/222)

"We urgently ask for a new residential school capable of housing at least 100 children." -Indians of the Piegan Reserve, 1946 (https://parl.canadiana.ca/view/oop.com_SOCHOC_2003_2_1/700)

"We are glad to have an Indian Residential School at Fort Vermillion, managed by a religious corporation. This is the only system which can satisfy us; and we hope this shall be maintained." -Chief Narcisse Pierrot, Beaver Indians of Boyer River Band, 1946 (https://parl.canadiana.ca/view/oop.com_SOCHOC_2003_2_1/224)

"We recommend that Indian Residential Schools be maintained as now operated and in the future be the centres where our orphan children be maintained therein." -Chief of Moose Woods, Charlie Hawke, 1947 (https://parl.canadiana.ca/view/oop.com_SOCHOC_2003_2_1/238)

"As we have already stated in 1939, since we are all Roman Catholic the teaching in these schools that we ask for should be given according to our religion and by teachers of our religion and we will accept none other." -Chief Dziedin, 1947 (https://parl.canadiana.ca/view/oop.com_SOCHOC_2003_2_1/568)

"We are all Catholics and we want the schools for our children to be of Catholic doctrine and to be taught by Catholic teachers. Only if the schools can be built closer to our homes we should be glad. The present Day and Residential School System has given good satisfaction." -Chief Andre Lacou, 1947 (https://parl.canadiana.ca/view/oop.com_SOCHOC_2003_2_1/196)

"Where unsuitable home conditions exist, Indian children should be removed from their parents just as white children are, when they are found to be neglected." -Indian Association of Alberta, 1947 (https://parl.canadiana.ca/view/oop.com_SOCHOC_2003_2_1/625)

"We are a band that is completely Catholic and our religion means a good deal to us. We are glad to be Catholic like over half the Indians in Canada are, and we want to stay that way. That's why we don't want to have the slightest thing to do with any kind of cheap public school. We insist on denominational schools and Catholic ones at that." -Chief Wahnapitae, 1946 (https://parl.canadiana.ca/view/oop.com_SOCHOC_2003_2_3/95)

"We Indians are naturally very religious. It was as far back as 1648 that the Jesuit Poneet came to this island and spent seven months with us teaching us the Catholic religion. We love our religion and mean to resist any attempts by minority groups to deprive us of it. For this reason we are very much opposed to the public system of education being foisted upon us. We want to keep our Catholic denominational schools and we wish to keep religion in our schools as we have always had it from the beginning." -Wikwemikong Reserve, 1946 (https://parl.canadiana.ca/view/oop.com_SOCHOC_2003_2_3/82)

"Our children are receiving the best education at the Pine Creek Residential School. They are receiving the best religious, academic and vocational training, which we greatly appreciate and for which we are grateful. We realizer the importance of good education now more than ever before. We especially realize the importance of religious teaching in our schools." -Chief Theadore Flatfoot, 1946 (https://parl.canadiana.ca/view/oop.com_SOCHOC_2003_2_1/572

"We, the Indians of Ohamil reserve submit the following demands to the Special Joint Committee in Ottawa . . . We believe the present system of education is satisfactory and no change is desired. We would like to see the present residential schools enlarged and new ones built." -Ohamil reserve, 1946 (https://parl.canadiana.ca/view/oop.com_SO CHOC_2003_2_1/184)

Fact #8: Not only are Indigenous parents and leaders are on record for wanting and even sometimes demanding specifically Christian residential schools, but people who didn't want them were called "fascists."

As I mentioned earlier, Christian missionaries had been reaching out to the natives for a very long time. In large numbers, the Indigenous people of Canada were persuaded to choose Christianity over their traditional religions. These missions were so successful that by 1899 a census showed that over 70% of Indigenous people in Canada identified as Christian.[15] It should be no surprise then, that we find records of Indigenous parents and leaders insisting so passionately, and in such large numbers, that their children's schools be Christian in the twentieth century.

In fact, you can read how the Indigenous peoples of Canada defended Christianity to the point that their leaders called people who wanted to change them "fascists." It's in the same official court documents:

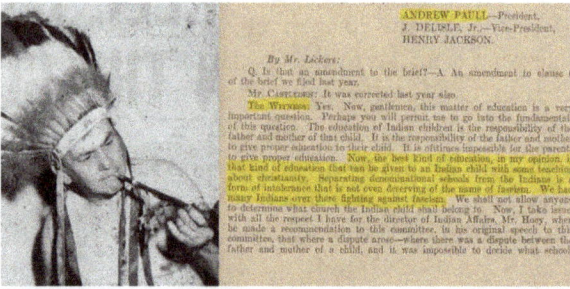

"Now, the best kind of education, in my opinion, is that kind of education that can be given with some teaching about Christianity. Separating denomination schools from the Indians is a form of intolerance that is not even deserving of the name of fascism." (https://parl.canadiana.ca/view/oop.com_SOCHOC_2003_2_2/255)

"Britain fought against religious control in the old country and so did many Indians; and with the vigour and energy that those Indians went over with to fight against that kind of fascism I stand here ready with as much courage as those boys that went over to fight against that." (https://parl.canadiana.ca/view/oop.com_SOCHOC_2003_2_2/256)

The debates were less about whether Christianity should be taught, and more about what kind of Christianity. They were also about who should teach it and who should have the power to make the decisions. Complaints were more about incompetence, power dynamics and bureaucracy. But there was little resistance to the teaching of Christianity itself.

Fact #9: There are official records of Indigenous parents and leaders criticizing residential schools for being too relaxed, and pressuring the government to increase discipline.

One thing you might have been told was that residential schools were unusually strict. What you might not have been told is that residential schools were often criticized for being too relaxed and giving too much freedom. Examples can be found in the same set of documents by searching for keywords like "residential school" and "discipline" in the Canadian Parliamentary Historical Records:

> As to education I have made it my business during my term as councillor and chief councillor to see what is wrong with Indian education. I have visited day schools and a small residential school there. My general experience is we have not got fully qualified teachers. During my term we have had good teachers. We have had really good teachers, and we have had really bad ones. It has gone down so bad that on one of my visits during school hours when I came into that room I saw the teacher at the desk taking a comb and combing the hair of a little pet terrier with the children flying around in the room throwing books at each other. I asked the teacher, "Is this recess time?" "No." "What is this? Is this a school or what?" "No, this is school hours." "But what has the dog got to do with it?" Well, I got down to red hot terms with the teacher. I threatened to fire her. She said, "You cannot do that. I am working for the Indian department." I said, "I will recommend you be fired." At the end of the term the Indian agent got rid of this lady. One or

> *INDIAN ACT* 421
>
> Mr. GIBSON: That is, the Indian day school.
>
> Canon ALDERWOOD: That is it. They said, we do not want our children to go to the day school; and he asked them, why. And they said because in the big school they teach them manners. When I questioned them as to what they meant by that and I found they appreciated the discipline which the children received in the boarding school and which they do not like to impose themselves, —as Indian parents do not like to do. And then further they told me this; one of the men present said I went to the commissioner about this matter, a group of us went, and told him that we wanted our children to go to the boarding school; but he said no, your children should go to the day school. Then one of them said, "I said to the commissioner we are a group of men who have been chosen from amongst our own people to come to you; why? Because we have a better education. Where did we get it? Everyone of us received it in the residential school and we want our children to go there too." Now, that was an actual example, in Alert Bay.

https://parl.canadiana.ca/view/oop.com_SOCHOC_2003_2_1/461

> very well. I know it was a matter of great concern to the agent. The discipline was simply shocking; as a matter of fact, there was no discipline at all. I asked the principal what his object was and he said he was trying to develop self expression. I said, "I imagine before long it will be out in the air because you will have no school left".
>
> The chief on this reserve is Chief Robert Marsden. He is a very fine type of man and has the only store on the reserve. He apparently has the support of the Indians and their confidence. He has a very fine musical band and they are fond of music. They go in for sports such as football, baseball and so on. I am now trying to skip along so I shall not be too long.
>
> The CHAIRMAN: I think you have now taken up your time, but with the unanimous consent of the committee you may continue.
>
> Mr. CASE: I think it was ten past when I started and I think it is now right on the thirty dot.
>
> The CHAIRMAN: It is all right, you have the unanimous consent of the committee.
>
> Mr. CASE: I wanted to deal with the schools and I have told you about them. Here, we had been log buildings which made rather picturesque little homes. Practically all were whitewashed. Usually they contained one room, but were very clean. We had an open forum afterwards which was attended by the men and women. I rather enjoyed listening to their discussion. They complained very bitterly about the discipline in this United Church school. One Indian offered the observation that when he played hooky from school his dad took the rod to him and that is the reason he had an education, but to-day the children just leave school whenever they like and nothing is done. I think that is something the department is well aware of and they are doing their best to correct that situation. Mr. Arneil was quite upset about the situation. It is

https://parl.canadiana.ca/view/oop.com_SOCHOC_2003_2_1/98

Parents also got together with their representatives and complained that children who came home from residential schools were so undisciplined that children would sometimes need to have discipline whipped into them by their fathers.

The government responded to these kinds of complaints and did their best to enact stricter disciplinary measures in residential schools over the coming decades.

Fact #10: Residential schools never became mandatory for Indigenous children. School attendance in general did. Prominent Indigenous leaders and representatives of the day advocated and supported the forceful removal of Indigenous children from their homes into residential schools.

It has been said that the government imposed residential schools on Indigenous peoples and forced children to attend. In reality, it was simply school in general that was made mandatory. It became mandatory for all children, not just Indigenous ones. Residential schools would only be mandatory for Indigenous children who had no other option, and who came from communities who either didn't want or weren't capable of opening schools of their own.[16] Often, these were places where there was much reported neglect and abuse. This is partially why even the Indigenous community supported the forced removal of children from their parents when necessary.

They agreed with the Canadian government that it was better for a child to be removed and sent to a Christian residential school for assimilation than to remain with their parents, where they might be neglected and either die, turn to crime or get caught up in cyclical poverty. Even the infamous "60's scoop" was conceived of by listening and responding to petitions of Indigenous leaders made in decades leading up to it:

Mr. Lickers: Well now, coming to education. At the bottom of page 15 of your brief, right at the last paragraph, at the bottom of the page you say, "Where unsuitable home conditions exist, Indian children should be removed from their parents just as white children are, when they are found to be neglected". Now who is going to be the governing authority there to decide whether or not children are neglected and whether they should be taken away from their parents.

Rev. Mr. Spence: A trained social worker can recommend to the Indian agent and the Indian agent can recommend to the inspector of the province and the inspector of the province can recommend to Ottawa and so right down from the top to the bottom.

Mr. Lickers: And where would these children be put?

Rev. Mr. Spence: Originally you know, the residential schools were for orphans who had no home. That is how these various residential schools in the different parts of our country came to be established. The original idea in the establishment of these residential schools was to provide a home for the children who had no proper home.

Mr. Lickers: I was just thinking you had better be rather cautious in submitting that line of argument in view of the evidence we have already had as to the poor condition of most of the Indians. We would not want some authorities to go in there and take all the children away.

children. I would like to know whether you are in favour of church schools or public schools?

The Witness: I am in favour of denominational schools. Now there should be residential schools where the Indians are nomadic, but there should be day schools where the Indians are stabilized in a particular reserve such as the Six Nations. In Kamloops the Indians are farmers and the children are attending day schools there, but the children should be taken out of the day schools and put into a residential school in that area.

Mr. Case: Are the day schools to be denominational?

The Witness: The schools should be denominational, yes.

Mr. Case: You are in favour of day schools being denominational?

The Witness: Yes, sir.

Fact #11: In general, Indigenous parents and leaders of the day who were opposed to residential schools opposed them because of the distance, not because of what was taught. Such parents preferred sending children to day schools instead of residential schools because they felt day schools led to more, not less, assimilation.

Cultural and religious assimilation wasn't very controversial back in those days. It was something many Indigenous leaders openly advocated for. Documents like these show that the main issue parents had with residential schools, besides the lack of discipline or funding, wasn't what was taught, but the long distances from home and rare visitations. Quite understandably, parents tended to prefer being closer to their children. There are actually records of residential school staff complaining about parents coming and camping out near the schools so they could see their children.[17] Parents weren't generally coming to take their children out of that kind of education system, but they did make petitions to the government to open day schools in their communities. Well funded residential schools that were close were preferred to day schools that were too far.

Parents missed their children. I think every mother or father can relate and sympathize with that. The Canadian government did, too. They tried to make some changes. Funding, however, was always difficult because much of this happened while wartime measures were in place, or during events like the Great Depression. There wasn't always a large budget. Christian charity didn't always cover everything either. That's the main reason why children often had to help out with work while at residential schools. Groundskeepers, maids and cooks were luxuries that were difficult to provide at the time.

Fact #12: In 1969, a time when there was frequently reported abuse, the Canadian government proposed to abolish the Indian Act, which would have meant total racial equality and the end of residential schools. Indigenous leaders, represented by Indigenous parents, strongly opposed it. So the schools remained open.

Today, a person might be accused of cultural genocide if they are in favor of the Indian Act and continuation of things like residential schools. But back then you'd be accused of it for wanting to abolish them. The Canadian government wanted and proposed abolishing the Indian act that residential schools were founded upon. Everyone would be equal. Indigenous people would be free to either embrace or move away from their traditional Indigenous culture, as they saw fit.[18]

> ". . . Presented to the First Session of the Twenty-eighth Parliament by the Honourable Jean Chrétien, Minister of Indian Affairs and Northern Development.
>
> To be an Indian is to be a man, with all a man's needs and abilities. To be an Indian is also to be different. It is to speak different languages, draw different pictures, tell different tales and to rely on a set of values developed in a different world.
>
> Canada is richer for its Indian component, although there have been times when diversity seemed of little value to many Canadians.
>
> But to be a Canadian Indian today is to be someone different in another way. It is to be

someone apart - apart in law, apart in the provision of government services and, too often, part in social contacts.

To be an Indian is to lack power - the power to act as owner of your lands, the power to spend your own money and, too often, the power to change your own condition.

Not always, but too often, to be an Indian is to be without - without a job, a good house, or running water; without knowledge, training or technical skill and, above all, without those feelings of dignity and self-confidence that a man must have if he is to walk with his head held high.

All these conditions of the Indians are the product of history and have nothing to do with their abilities and capacities. Indian relations with other Canadians began with special treatment by government and society, and special treatment has been the rule since Europeans first settled in Canada. Special treatment has made of the Indians a community disadvantaged and apart.

Obviously, the course of history must be changed.

To be an Indian must be to be free - free to develop Indian cultures in an environment of legal, social and economic equality with other Canadians...

The Government believes that its policies must lead to the full, free and non-discriminatory participation of the Indian people in Canadian society. Such a goal requires a break with the past. It requires that the Indian people's role of dependence be replaced by a role of equal status, opportunity and responsibility, a role they can share with all other Canadians.

This proposal is a recognition of the necessity made plain in a year's intensive discussions with Indian people throughout Canada. The Government believes that to continue its past course of action would not serve the interests of either the Indian people or their fellow Canadians.

The policies proposed recognize the simple reality that the separate legal status of Indians and the policies which have flowed from it have kept the Indian people apart from and behind other Canadians. The Indian people have not been full citizens of the communities and provinces in which they live and have not enjoyed the equality and benefits that such participation offers.

The treatment resulting from their different status has been often worse, sometimes equal and occasionally better than that accorded to their fellow citizens. What matters is that it has been different.

Many Indians, both in isolated communities and in cities, suffer from poverty. The discrimination which affects the poor, Indian and non-Indian alike, when compounded with a legal status that sets the Indian apart, provides dangerously fertile ground for social and cultural discrimination.

In recent years there has been a rapid increase in the Indian population. Their health and education levels have improved. There has been a corresponding rise in expectations that the structure of separate treatment cannot meet.

A forceful and articulate Indian leadership has

developed to express the aspirations and needs of the Indian community. Given the opportunity, the Indian people can realize an immense human and cultural potential that will enhance their own well-being, that of the regions in which they live and of Canada as a whole. Faced with a continuation of past policies, they will unite only in a common frustration.

The Government does not wish to perpetuate policies which carry with them the seeds of disharmony and disunity, policies which prevent Canadians from fulfilling themselves and contributing to their society. It seeks a partnership to achieve a better goal. The partners in this search are the Indian people, the governments of the provinces, the Canadian community as a whole and the Government of Canada. As all partnerships do, this will require consultation, negotiation, give and take, and co- operation if it is to succeed.

Many years will be needed. Some efforts may fail, but learning comes from failure and from what is learned success may follow. All the partners have to learn; all will have to change many attitudes.

Governments can set examples, but they cannot change the hearts of men. Canadians, Indians and non-Indians alike stand at the crossroads. For Canadian society the issue is whether a growing element of its population will become full participants contributing in a positive way to the general well-being or whether, conversely, the present social and economic gap will lead to their increasing frustration and isolation, a threat to the general well- being of society. For many Indian people, one road does exist, the only road that has existed since Confederation and before, the road of different status, a road which has led to a blind alley of deprivation and frustration. This road, because it is a separate road, cannot lead to full participation, to equality in practice as well as in theory. In the pages which follow, the Government has outlined a number of measures and a policy which it is convinced will offer another road for Indians, a road that would lead gradually away from different status to full social, economic and political participation in Canadian life. This is the choice. Indian people must be persuaded, must persuade themselves, that this path will lead them to a fuller and richer life.

Canadian society as a whole will have to recognize the need for changed attitudes and a truly open society. Canadians should recognize the dangers of failing to strike down the barriers which frustrate Indian people. If Indian people are to become full members of Canadian society they must be warmly welcomed by that society.

The Government commends this policy for the consideration of all Canadians, Indians and non-Indians, and all governments in Canada..."

- Statement of the Government of Canada on Indian Policy

This was done in the same spirit of equality as the civil rights movement happening in The United States at the time. The difference was that, in Canada, these ideas of civil rights and equality were rejected by the parents and leaders of the people they would be extended to. As a result, institutions like residential schools had to remain open.

Fact #13: There have been many reports of positive experiences in residential schools that you can read.

"You may have heard stories from 7,000 witnesses in the process that were negative," says residential school attendee Tomson Highway. "But what you haven't heard are the 7,000 reports that were positive stories. There are many very successful people today that went to those schools and have brilliant careers and are very functional people, very happy people like myself. I have a thriving international career, and it wouldn't have happened without that school." [19] Similar sentiments have been reported in letters that many have tried to ignore and cover up.

I'll end with some quotations of just a few examples. I would like to stress that I believe these positive testimonies in no way justify abuses which took place in these schools. If even one child were abused, it would be one too many. But I hope you'll consider them, along with the rest of these facts, when reflecting on this question of cultural genocide. Thanks again for writing in!

"Letters to Senator Beyak"

"As retired educators ourselves, with a combined experience of 26 years in Aboriginal and Metis schools, we witnessed first-hand the positive anecdotes and experiences of those who gained from their attendance at Residential Schools. Unfortunately, current orthodoxy forces their 'voices' to be silenced."

"As the brother of a nun who worked in the system, and the nephew of a Jesuit who worked there too, I categorically refuse to believe that all the people who worked in these schools were as evil as they are being portrayed to be. Indeed, they were seeking, under the social rules that were generally accepted at the time, to do good and to help these children."

"I worked with Chipewyan people as an employee of the Catholic Church from 1991 to 2001. . . I heard many positive comments by native people who had attended residential school in Fort Resolution. . . One woman, a Chief of her community for some years, said, 'I couldn't wait to go back to residential school. You were clean and you had good food.' I knew another family, eight children. The Dad was a trapper who spent the winter on the barren lands. His wife contracted TB and was placed in the isolation hospital in Ft. Res. The children were taken by the Dad each year to the school to keep them safe. It was very hard for the youngest who was only 4 yrs at the time – traumatic even to be separated from parents and older sibs. However, the child survived where otherwise he may not have. The schools must be viewed in the context of the social and economic circumstances at the time."

"My husband has worked and lived in several aboriginal communities in the north which greatly benefited from these schools and where the people speak very highly of the care and instruction they received. We are only given one side of the story."

"I spent over ten years living and working on reserves and northern settlements. And I remember, as a teacher, how often we had to convince the population to keep their children at home and go to the Day School, rather than to send them to a residential school. If the residential schools had been so bad why were parents insisting that their children go? I personally saw a lot of good emanate from these schools. I do admit mistakes were made but those same mistakes also existed in the population at large. Yes, most people were well intentioned and worked with the knowledge they thought best."

"I have lived and worked in Prince Albert, SK, for a number of years and had the opportunity to meet retired teachers of residential schools, and listen to their experiences as well. Those I met, were all good, hardworking and well intentioned people. I also had the opportunity to meet First Nations people, teachers and lawyers, who are now effective leaders and advocates among and on behalf of their people, exactly because they received education in those residential schools."

"I attended a First Nations Art Exhibition in Fort McMurray and I met a native artist who told me how grateful she was to the nuns and priests in her community who ran the school because for her it was a place of refuge. She said that her parents would go out on the trap-line and leave them to fend for themselves and she would go sit on the steps of the school and hope someone would help her."

"I myself am a product of a Catholic convent school and while some people who attended that school with me will now say that the nuns were racists and treated them unfairly, that was not my experience. Yes, they were strict, but the principles of kindness and consideration for others were held in high esteem and they instilled in me values that successfully took me through more than 40 years in the business world."

"My mother has a cousin who attended a residential school and whenever she is asked about it she tells her that her experience was a good one, in fact she credits the residential school system with having provided her the opportunity to have a good education. Her experience in residential school was so good that when the federal government offered a blanket cash settlement to all former attendees, she refused to take it."

"I know from first-hand experience that the Residential schools provided a lot of good and back in the fifties it gave children from the reserves the opportunity to witness life off the reserve, to be educated in more than a one room school house for all, and to join in social programs to broaden their experience."

"I think of the many people who provided clothing and funding to help ensure the children had a good experience at the Residential school while away from home. I am not naive enough to suggest that in some areas there weren't some serious problems which should never have happened but you cannot tarnish the whole system with the same brush."

"Having worked for and with Aboriginal people in northwestern Ontario – many who are my friends – I support what you have said. Are there not two sides to this story? Why is only one side being expressed? Shame on our government."

"I grew up on a Residential school, and although some aspects of it were hard, I also found the provincial public school even harder. I can never forget the violence of Canadian public schools. One indigenous boy was beaten up so bad by a white boy in my high school, that he was hospitalized. The school did nothing. I was assaulted on the school bus. Bus driver did nothing. No one got beaten in the residential school I attended. Corporal punishment was almost unheard of. My very worst memories of school was that of the provincial public schools and their strap-happy principals. I have never seen such hypocrisy as a government official apologizing. Secretly they are only glad that they have spun the public mind set to having the churches take on the blame and responsibility the governments should be shouldering." [20]

"School Days: The Residential School Experience"

". . . The schools were not absolutely destructive. Between 2009 and 2011, many students have come forward to express their gratitude to former teachers at the Truth and Reconciliation Commission events. Their testimony is a reminder that not all residential school experiences are identical. Although few students went to residential school willingly, once they were there, there were activities—sports, arts, reading, dancing, writing—that many students came to enjoy. Even after they were old enough to leave, some chose to stay in school and complete their education. In certain cases, students developed lifelong relationships with their former teachers. Others not only finished high school, they pursued post-secondary education. Some went on to take leadership positions in Aboriginal organizations, the churches, and in society at large. Despite the shortcomings of the system, some students were able to adjust to it, and others achieved significant accomplishments.

These positive experiences stand in the shadow of the system's overall failings, but they are also part of the residential school story. Children who faced difficult home situations sometimes have more positive assessments of residential schools. In 1944 twelve-year-old Rita Joe, an orphan, was living with relatives who alternately abused and neglected her. Fearful, she called the Indian agent and asked if he could arrange to have her admitted to the Shubenacadie school in Nova Scotia. Joe acknowledged that many negative things happened at the school, but she never regretted going there.

In 1956, as a young mother with four children under six years of age, she and her husband Frank decided to send their oldest daughter to Shubenacadie. 'We knew she would get an education there, and would be cared for until we were better off.' Like Rita and Frank Joe, many other parents used residential schools as part of a family survival strategy. Louis Calihoo, a Métis man who went north to the Klondike in 1898 to make money during the Gold Rush, placed his sons in the Grouard school.

During the Great Depression of the 1930s, a Chilcotin father wrote his son in residential school, 'I didn't make much money this year, just enough to buy grub to live on. You are lucky to be in school where you get plenty to eat. If you were home you would get hungry many days.' Florence Bird was born to Métis parents in Fort Chipewyan in 1899. After the death of her father Joseph in 1909, she was raised in the Holy Angels Convent at Fort Chipewyan. A sickly child, she thought she would not have survived without the convent. 'There were lots of pitiful kids in those days. The orphans were more pitiful than everybody else because they were badly treated by the people and even by the relatives sometimes.'

Although the nuns were strict, she thought that with so many children to supervise, they had few options. Martha Mercredi was another orphaned Métis child who was raised in Holy Angels. 'I was never lonely because I took to the nuns as my own relatives. Sister Superior was my grandmother and Sister Lucy was the teacher and she was like my momma, she's the one that's my guardian. So I have no complaint about the convent. I am very glad that they showed me how to read and write.' Students involved in sports, music, drama, and dance found that these activities helped them maintain a sense of their own value, and were sources of strength in later life. Andrew Amos recalled that at the Kamloops school, 'The treatment was good as long as you excelled in sports.' He went on to become a provincial boxing champion.

Travelling to fights and games allowed students to leave the school and see other parts of the province. Amos recalled, 'It was through competitive sports, and the girls with their dancing and travel, that we were able to cope and survive the daily routine of life at the residential school.' Even if they were poorly equipped, residential school hockey, football, and baseball teams provided many students with a refuge and a source of pride. Alex, a student at the St.-Marc-deFiguery school in Amos,

Quebec, said, 'At the residential school, if it wasn't for hockey, I would have gone crazy. Sport became my support. Until I was thirty years old, I played and when I was on the ice, I would let it all out.' The prejudices of the day meant that girls enjoyed fewer athletic opportunities.

The Kamloops school was known for its dance program. Vivian Ignace, one of the dancers, had mixed feelings about her experience, noting that dancers were not allowed to participate in sports for fear of injury. Despite this, she concluded that 'through that experience with the Kamloops Indian Residential School Dancers, I learned some assertiveness skills. I learned to smile even when I wasn't happy. I learned to get along and talk with people and that was good. I learned a lot through that Irish nun.'

Some students were grateful for the religious instruction they received. Edna Gregoire, who attended the Kamloops school, for example, said, 'My experience at the residential school was good. That's one thing I'll tell you, it was really good to be able to go to school and to learn how to read and write. And the other thing, the best of all, I was happy to learn about God.' Margaret Stonechild recalled the File Hills, Saskatchewan, principal as a very good religious instructor. 'I am eternally grateful for that because I have a firm standing in Christian beliefs to this day.' Bernard Pinay said that at File Hills, he never felt religion was being forced down his throat. Some parents, at the urging of missionaries, sent their children to residential school specifically for a religious education. In some cases, strong personal relationships developed between students and staff. Eleanor Brass's parents, Fred and Marybelle Dieter, were married at the File Hills boarding school where Kate Gillespie, the principal, and her sister Janet (the school matron) made the wedding arrangements, and baked the wedding cake.

Shirley Bear recalled one principal of the Prince Albert school as a tyrant. However, 'The next principal, Rev. A.J. Serase, was an angel. After he came, the whole system changed. He was just like a father to the students. He was the minister who married my husband and me.' Many students, either on their own or with the encouragement of a well-remembered teacher, developed a love of learning. Jane Willis, at the Anglican school at Fort George on James Bay, credits her decision to complete her education to one of her teachers, who worked hard to develop students' self-confidence. 'Learning was a pleasure with Mr. Woods as our cheerleader and coach. He urged us to ask questions, to take an active part in class instead of sitting back and taking his word for everything.' At the Moose Factory School in Ontario, Billy Diamond became a voracious reader. When the time came for him to move on to high school in Sault Ste. Marie, he saw it as an opportunity for adventure, learning, and meeting new friends. Once there, he helped form an Indian student council. Diamond went on, as leader of the James Bay Cree, to negotiate the 1975 James Bay and Northern Quebec Agreement, Canada's first comprehensive land-claims agreement. While the residential school experience left him feeling embarrassed about his culture, Peter Irniq described the education he received in Chesterfield Inlet as 'top-notch.' 'As much as that particular teacher used to call us bloody dodos and no good for nothing, a bunch of hounds of iniquity, he taught us pretty good in terms of English...” [21]

"Letter to Sun Columnist"
By Jim Bissell

"... The time has come for 70 year old people like me to speak the truth. a little background. I grew up surrounded by 4 reserves and a large community of indigenous peoples (95%). It was a community of wonderful, kind, very generous, very humorous people that remained that way even when very poor. Also I have a wonderful successful indigenous daughter with grandkids and great granddaughters. I am not a Catholic and I do not belong to any church. I belong to me and my family but I like Christian values.

It should be noted that the missionaries though were very essential to our success in the northern communities at that time. I had my first TB test administered by a missionary trying to stop a TB outbreak. (I hated her at the time for the scratches on my back. LOL). I got my first stitches from a wonderful nun. I got my first tooth pulled by a missionary. My first X-ray by the nuns. My first teacher was an angel called Sister Rita. I will never forget her and her deep love of all the children she met and taught over the years. My best teacher ever and she was not qualified by Government standards. So although I have never been a Catholic, their church has been very good for me and although I now do know of one very bad priest, most of the people were wonderful. I can still see brother Fillion who later became a priest working all by himself outside the school window making a wonderful merry-go-round for the school yard.

There also were two residential schools in the community. When I arrived in the community, there were no phones, very poor roads, mostly winter access, and not a lot of services other than the churches. The mission school was there long before my time. It has been told to me by elders that many small children, some way younger than school age, were dropped off at the missions sick, hoping the nuns could heal them. Sad to say many died from measles, diphtheria, TB, smallpox, flu and many other conditions of the poor. Just the reality of the north. Years ago most of the dead were placed in the trees so the birds and other animals could take them back to nature.

It was the churches that convinced them that that part of their culture should be changed so that to stop the spread of disease so they started to bury the dead. If the dead were Christians, their grave was marked by a painted rock of a small wooden cross which rotted away in 25 years or so. No one could afford a headstone and if they could there was no one that made them at the time. Times were hard and in fact desperate in the 30,s Many people owed their lives to the missionaries and we tend to forget that. They were not always right, no of course not, but they actually wanted to educate, feed and make the lives of all people better regardless of where they came from. The churches do not need to apologize for trying to educate the poor in the only system that would work for nomadic peoples, they need to say sorry though for protecting and moving about the few bad apples (priests).

The Government saying they are sorry is meaningless. They didn't have a clue of the impact of their decisions at the time and they don't have now. Most of the older generation that did suffer are long dead and gone or have forgiven. It seems to me that many of the new generation just want to be victims and feel money would solve their pain. We need to understand that very few people wanted to live in the north under the isolated conditions at the time just to help out with a few indigenous peoples. After the federal government took over the school system, most of my junior high school teachers were immigrants from the British Commonwealth (India, England Ireland and other countries) as no Alberta teachers wanted to live up there when they could live in or near a city with a doctor, bank, good grocery store, ambulance and my goodness even Policeman. The quality of my education suffered because all of a sudden the nuns were not qualified to teach us in 1967 thus I had to try and take lessons from teachers with a very heavy accent and hard to understand and wanting to move close to the cities as soon as they could. Thank goodness the missionaries were there for the past 300 years. Were they all good? No, but many were wonderful and now that seems to be forgotten.

How many of today's critics have relatives that went up to those communities in those times to try and help? Not many, I bet. The media today is only telling half the story, so I feel we as witnesses have to speak up and speak to the truth. If you want I will take you to a sacred ground where hundreds of people were left in the ramps and trees or layed on the ground when they died. No one but historical memory marked their graves.

Please believe me when I say that the missionaries were not a bunch of evil persons out to kill little children like it sounds in today's media. That is not what I witnessed. The missionaries knew that the ancient peoples of our land could not continue to exist in a nomadic and isolated society, so they tried to educate them and of course change their culture to be more compatible with the conditions of the times. Were they right? Maybe, I don't know, but at least they were willing to try and help.

Like I tell my children, I cannot become indigenous like them but they can become Canadians like me and they are. There are more success stories out there than even you realize. The missionaries did not just throw bodies into the ground. Most were marked by a small wooden cross made by the brothers of the mission or parents of the child. Those crosses are long gone. Sad but true. I can also take you to the unmarked graves of many people that were not indigenous as well if you want. That was the way of the north.

Sorry to ramble on for so long but many things need to be said and if the elders of our society lack the moral courage to say them, we are doomed anyway. Please encourage people to stand up and be heard for the good not just the bad. . ." [22]

Former Dene Chief Cece Hodgson-McCauley:

"We all heard of horrible lies created by some individuals in order to receive as much money as they could." [23]

"I spent 10 years there, going home every summer for the holidays on the mission boat. . . The nuns taught us so much. I only remember one nun who was very strict and one nun who made us pray too much. In every society you have people with personalities that are on the bad side. . . But I can swear on the Bible that my time in the convent was good. We ate three meals a day, not fancy but nourishing, a lot of recreation, every winter they built us a big slide and we would have fun sliding and we went on many picnics in summer time and in the winter we would go for hay rides, sleighs pulled by oxen. . . We set rabbit snares and ate rabbit. They had pemmican, that is pounded meat that natives love. They taught us how to knit stockings for ourselves, to do fancy beading for moccasins and to do quill work, from two quills up to 12 quills. We learned to make our own dresses, they taught how to cook and bake and clean. . . The boys had hockey and baseball. The native Indian boys used to always try to beat the Metis boys, lots of fun. . . My family says the same thing, my sister swears by it. . . We were treated wonderfully. . . For a lot of poor kids, it was the only place people could get three square meals a day. . ." [24]

"An Open Letter to the Primate of the Anglican Church of Canada"
By Rodney A. Clifton

". . . On March 20, 2017 you, the Most Rev. Fred Hiltz, along with national Indigenous Anglican Bishop, Mark MacDonald, and the General Secretary, Archdeacon Michael Thompson, published an open letter addressed to Senator Lynn Beyak in response to a speech she gave in a Senate committee meeting.

I simply remind you that Senator Beyak said there were *some* good things that happened in Indian residential schools (IRS), a point I thought would *not* be controversial, at least not to the extent that you, as the Primate of the Anglican Church, would feel a need to attack what she said. The claim she made is true because there is considerable evidence for her claim in the Truth and Reconciliation (TRC) Report itself, and there is even further evidence in an op-ed that Senator Murray Sinclair published in the *Calgary Herald* a couple of years earlier.

Despite this evidence, you said in your letter to Senator Beyak that there was "nothing good" about the IRS system. As an Anglican who has carefully read the TRC Report and Senator Sinclair's op-ed, and as a person who spent some time in residential schools, I find your assertion troubling. Let me explain why.

Reading your message to Senator Beyak brought back memories of a letter I received more than 50 years earlier. In August 1966, I was boarding at Old Sun, the Anglican residential school on the Siksika First Nation (Blackfoot Reserve) in southern Alberta. I received a letter offering me a position as the senior boys' supervisor at Stringer Hall, the Anglican residential hostel in Inuvik, NWT, for the 1966-67 year. I welcomed this job offer, in part because it would help me better understand Indian and Eskimo students, and partly because I could save money to continue with my university studies, paying for tuition, books, and room and board.

Two years earlier, in 1964, I had begun my teacher training in the Faculty of Education at the University of Alberta. After completing my first year in the BEd program, I joined a small group of students in a new cross-cultural program preparing teachers to work in Canada's North and in schools on Métis colonies and First Nations reserves. The student teachers in this program were required to complete a summer internship, and I was assigned to the Blackfoot Reserve, 100 kilometers east of Calgary.

From the beginning of May to the end of August, I worked in the agency office as a "go-for- it" (the male staff members, Indigenous and non-Indigenous, called me a "swamper") whose job was assisting the office staff. I also did other jobs on the reserve: registering children for kindergarten, acting as a truancy officer, working with local ranchers baling hay and branding calves, helping erect teepees for the Sun Dance, helping with handing out the $5 treaty money at Treaty Days, and many other things that would expand my under-standing of Aboriginal people. I was truly fortunate because a local family, the Ayoungman family, "adopted" me, inviting me to their home and to their family gatherings, Indian Days, rodeos, and Sunday picnics.

During that summer, I stayed in a room in the teachers' wing at Old Sun. When I arrived in May, there were Siksika students in residence, but at the end of June, there were only five people living at the school: the Anglican priest, the Rev. R. F. Brown, the three Rosesting girls—young orphaned Cree children from Hobbema—and me. Hilda Red Gun, a local Siksika woman, worked at the school during the day to make meals and to care for the little girls.

By the beginning of August—three months into my internship—Indian Affairs had still not paid me the modest stipend promised, so I had to make some money before returning to university. Seeing an advertisement in the *Anglican Journal*, I applied for the senior boys' position at Stringer Hall, and, as you can imagine, I welcomed the letter offering me the job.

Following my summer work on the Blackfoot Reserve, the residential supervisor's position in Inuvik was exactly what I needed to further my understanding of Aboriginal culture. In addition, I would be able to save enough money to return to university. It was, as you will see, a fascinating experience, and I took copious notes and photographs, all of which have been filed with the National Centre for Truth and Reconciliation at the University of Manitoba.

In late August, I boarded an old DC-4 at the municipal airport in Edmonton. Twelve hours later, after many stops at small communities along the Mackenzie River, I arrived at the Inuvik airport, where I was met by the hostel administrator, the Rev. Leonard Holman. We drove to the community of Inuvik, and I settled into my small bedroom, situated between two dorm rooms in Stringer Hall, the Anglican hostel.

The next day, I toured the building and received my job description: supervising 85 senior boys, between the ages of 12 and about 21, housed in three dormitory rooms, for six days a week. I would be responsible for these boys for some 22 hours a day. Of course, on most days I did not supervise boys during school hours, but if students were too ill to go to school but not sick enough to be in the hostel infirmary, they remained in the dormitories where I was responsible for them. As it turned out, two or three times a week, I was up at various times during the night, looking after boys who were ill or who were being bothered by other boys. Because the children's home communities were often far away, most of the students remained in residence on weekends and during the Christmas and Easter breaks. Very soon, I realized that the year was going to be very demanding, yet I thought it would be interesting—and indeed, it was a year I have never forgotten.

Within a few days, students began arriving to reside in the hostel. Some came by aircraft from small coastal communities such as Tuktoyaktuk, Sachs Harbour, and Cambridge Bay; others came by boat and aircraft from communities along the Mackenzie River, including Aklavik, Fort McPherson, and Fort Good Hope.

I do not recall any of the young children crying

at night because they were lonely. Rather, the new arrivals, especially the Inuit children, were quite stoic and reserved, hesitant to interact with children and adults they did not know. I remember that while the Inuit children were very shy but excited about going to school, the Dene, Métis, and Caucasian children were much more outgoing and noisier. In fact, some Dene boys were quite aggressive toward Inuit boys. Rev. Holman and his wife, who was the matron, welcomed all the children with kindness and, indeed, with a considerable dose of love. The older children quickly found friends and relatives as students decided which beds they would have and who would sleep next to them.

One of the obvious signs of the difficulties that young children have in adapting to new and strange environments is bed-wetting. But, as my notes indicate, bed-wetting was infrequent, and when it occurred, it mostly happened after the children had watched a movie in the gymnasium, stayed up later than normal, and consumed soft drinks.

We now know that many children were physically and sexually abused in residential schools, both by other students and by staff members. Such abuse of children is clearly reprehensible, and all adults, Aboriginal or non-Aboriginal, who preyed upon or brutalized children, should be punished for their crimes. So should any administrators from both the churches and the Department of Indian and Northern Affairs who covered up these crimes. But at the same time, innocent people who worked in Indian Residential Schools (IRS) and those who instructed these children should *not* be maligned with false accusations. Many of them should, in fact, be honoured by their respective churches for the service they provided to these children.

Returning to the story of my life at Stringer Hall, by the beginning of September, when classes began at the nearby Sir Alexander Mackenzie School, about 280 students were in residence: 73 percent were Inuit, 16 percent were Dene, and 12 percent were Caucasian and Métis. A similar number of students resided in Grollier Hall, the Roman Catholic hostel, but there were fewer Inuit, more Dene, and about the same percentage of Caucasian and Métis students in that hostel. Strangely, the TRC Report does not mention that, in the Far North, all students, Aboriginal and non-Aboriginal, went to a residential institution if their homes were in small communities without day schools.

Also, the Report does not state that some of the children arrived at Stringer Hall in September wearing the same school clothing they wore when they went home in the spring, not having bathed or changed in two months. Some of these children had been standing in smudge fires, trying to escape the hordes of blood-sucking insects, and a number had arrived with infected bug bites on their scalps. A few children arrived with ear infections so severe that pus was running down their necks. At the beginning of the year, these children cried themselves to sleep. As you might expect, the priority of the residential school staff, particularly the nursing sister, was to clean up the children and treat their infections.

To put the students' living conditions and infections into context, anyone reading this account needs to realize that it wasn't until the early 1950s that a weekly bath with a change of clothes became the norm for most urban Canadians. For people living on farms and in small communities where water had to be hand-pumped from wells and heated on coal and wood stoves, a bath with a change of clothing was a luxury reserved for special occasions. In the North, it was even more difficult to bathe and change clothing, especially for the children who were with their parents living in tents at hunting and fishing camps.

There is little doubt that the hostel children appreciated ending a busy week with a hot shower, clean pajamas, and a chance to slip between clean sheets in their very own beds, just as other Canadian children did. Having the children bathe, get their hair cut by older boys, and put on clean institutional clothing is now called "cultural genocide," a phrase that completely distorts what we were doing at the time—keeping children clean, well-fed, and healthy.

One story clearly illustrates the kind of treatment the children received. A few days after I arrived, a young woman walked into the staff dining room. Her name was Rosaline Mallick, and she was the new residential nurse. Her clothes were strange, and by her accent we knew she wasn't Canadian. Over dinner, she told us that she had come from London, England, to be our "nursing sister."

IN DEFENSE OF OUR CHURCHES 57

To the surprise of many Canadians on staff, this 22-year-old woman had come from the centre of the British Commonwealth to one of its most distant outposts, from a warm autumn day in England to a cold, dark, and bleak August evening 300 miles north of the Arctic Circle, from a major world city to a small isolated community hugging the east bank of the Mackenzie River. She told us that she was going to work in the hostel as part of her Christian service. All of us were astounded by her commitment to work with Aboriginal children.

In early December, when the sun had already sunk below the southern horizon, a senior boy, John, complained that he was too sick to attend school. I was not surprised, given his peaky appearance. As might be expected, some boys would sometimes feign illness so they could get a day off from classes, but this young man was not one of those who tried to avoid going to school.

After sending the other 84 students to breakfast in the dining room and going to John's bed—one of 60 in the largest dorm—I helped him climb the stairs to the second floor, and together we shuffled along the hall to the infirmary.

"Miss Mallick," I said, "I have brought John because he is extremely sick. I know you're on your way to breakfast, but could you please look at him?" Immediately, she began asking John questions about his symptoms.

I left John in Miss Mallick's care and went down for breakfast. Besides being responsible for this 12-year-old, I had to ensure that the other boys got fed, went back to the dorms, straightened up their beds, brushed their teeth, put on their parkas and mukluks, and went off to school.

At about 11 a.m., Miss Mallick came to the senior boys' dorms and found me sorting clothing. Clean clothing was stored in each boy's numbered cubicle—1 to 100—in a locked storeroom, and sorting clothing was an important and time-consuming part of my job. Of course, the easiest way of sorting and storing clothing for 85 boys was to assign numbered cubicles to each boy so that the numbers of the cubicles matched the numbers on their clothing. (Even my clothing had a number). These numbers were never used to refer to any of the boys in the residence, not even for those children with long and difficult Indigenous names.

Nurse Mallick told me that John probably had appendicitis and that she had helped Rev. Holman take him to the hospital. At coffee break that afternoon, she told the staff that a doctor had phoned to say that John's appendix had burst and emergency surgery had just finished.

After a few hours in the recovery room, she said, John would be transferred to a general ward, and people could visit him in a day or two. In fact, many staff members and students did exactly that over the next few days.

Another story illustrates the dedication that staff members gave to the children in their charge. In that same early December, I spotted a man cross-country skiing with a group of children on a trail behind Grollier Hall, the Roman Catholic hostel. The next day, during my two-hour break from residential duties, I walked over to the ski hut and met Fr. Jean-Marie Mouchet, the Catholic priest who was teaching these northern children to cross-country ski. I told him that I was the senior boys' supervisor at Stringer Hall, and a cross-country skier myself, having grown up in Jasper.

When I asked Fr. Mouchet if I could ski with his club, he said that I could use the trails, and that I should tell the Anglican students that if they wanted to learn to ski, he would equip and teach them. My parents sent my skis to Inuvik, and several the Anglican children from Stringer Hall joined Fr. Mouchet's ski club, using skis, boots, and poles donated by the Roman Catholic Church. The ecumenical co- operation was, I think, something to celebrate both then and now.

That was my introduction to Fr. Mouchet, a ski coach about whom Canada would soon hear more. I recall seeing students from Grollier Hall—Peter Allen, Sharon and Shirley Firth, and Jeanette Tourangeau—out on the ski trail in those cold dark days in December and January. Fr. Mouchet had strung electric lights through the trees above the trail, lights which were certainly needed when the sun was below the horizon during those days in the dead of winter.

I will never forget something Fr. Mouchet told me late one afternoon as we watched the children returning from a 90-minute training run: "All these children need is to learn to overcome themselves, and then nothing can stop them." He believed that these Indigenous students could determine the way their lives unfolded.

He was, of course, correct. In a few years, a number of these Aboriginal skiers became members of the Canadian national cross- country ski team, winning medals across North America and around Europe, and representing Canada in the 1972 Winter Olympics in Sapporo, Japan. Imagine what it was like for these Aboriginal children to be learning how to cross-country ski in Inuvik in 1966 and then six years later to be representing their country at the Olympic games in Japan.

Many people seem to be unaware that some residential school employees were Aboriginals, and this was true at both Old Sun and Stringer Hall. At Stringer Hall, for example, two of the six supervisors were young Inuit women, Annie and Lucy, who, contrary to considerable testimony in the TRC Report, spoke to the young Inuit children in their mother tongue. Mrs. Thomas, a Dene woman who was the school's seamstress, made parkas and mukluks for the children and lived in the hostel with her four-year-old daughter. She spoke both English and her native language to the Dene children, but most of the Dene and Métis children spoke English upon their arrival.

In general, the relationships between staff and students were very cordial and often friendly. There were, of course, tense and even agitated moments because the children were often cooped up in the residence on Saturdays and Sundays when blizzards were blowing outside. At times, staff members, who never got enough sleep, could be irritable, especially if children were ill during the night. Sometimes, students squabbled among themselves. The Dene boys often treated the Inuit boys in condescending ways, picking on them and calling them unacceptable names. As the supervisor, my job was to calm these situations and keep all the boys treating each other with respect.

The young children, the junior boys and girls, loved spending time with some of the staff members. I remember with great fondness some of the Inuit children coming to my room on Saturday afternoons to take Nurse Mallick and me for walks. Often, we would climb the hill behind the hostel so the children could slide down the snow-covered road on cardboard boxes. At other times, we walked out on the ice of the Mackenzie River, carefully avoiding the dog sled trails used by people going to trap lines and hunting camps, or travelling between communities. The children knew how dangerous dog teams could be because they had either heard about or seen people who had been attacked by dogs. During that very winter, as her parents watched in horror, a young girl had been killed by a dog team on a trail close to Fort McPherson. Life in the North was tough and precarious, and these children knew it.

During our winter walks, I would practice the Inuktitut expressions the children had taught me. I had told some of the five- and six-year-old children that if they taught me to speak Inuktitut, I would help them learn English. By February, the children, who were always polite and respectful, could speak rudimentary English, but all I could say were a few Inuktitut phrases—and they were of the taboo variety!

Predictably, the children encouraged me to say these naughty phrases and found my speech very amusing. "Funny, funny, Mr. Clifton," they would giggle. The little girls would turn their backs on me, cover their mouths with their hands and laugh quietly, their dark eyes dancing with glee as they held onto each other. I called this group "the giggling girls," thus teaching them a new English expression, one that they appreciated when I teased them by saying, "Oh no, here are the giggling girls coming to take me for a walk! I had better get my parka and mukluks on."

The Indigenous and non-Indigenous adults I knew in the Anglican residential schools genuinely wanted to help the children receive a good education to prepare them for the modern world. Most were caring people, but a couple of the older supervisors were cranky and tired, probably because they had been supervising large groups of children for many years. These older supervisors also clung to the idea that strict discipline was the only way to keep children from taking the wrong path. But to the best of my memory, most staff members were trying to fulfil the evangelistic calling of committed Christians: to help the poor, tend to the weak, and treat the sick.

Archbishop Hiltz, I must tell you that my mind was filled with these fond memories when I read your open letter to Senator Beyak. With deep respect to you and the Church, I think your letter ignores and even denies the work and the love that Nurse Mallick and the thousands of other Anglicans gave to numerous Indigenous children. If there was nothing good about the residential school system, how would you describe what Nurse Mallick did in saving the life of that 12-year-old Inuit boy? Had John been out at the hunting camp with his parents, no matter how much they loved him, he surely would have died a painful death.

The TRC Report references the sad reality that 3,201 children died while enrolled in residential schools and hostels, most of them from infectious diseases like tuberculosis and influenza. The death of any child is, of course, dreadful to contemplate. But surprisingly, there is no discussion—not one word in the TRC Report—about the countless children like John whose lives were saved because residential school staff looked after them, loved them, and cared for them. Likewise, there is no mention of the innumerable children with infected bug bites whom Nurse Mallick and the many other dedicated medical professionals treated. Likewise, there is no recognition of hundreds of six-year-olds who immediately received treatment for their eardrums, which were so badly infected that green smelly pus was running down their necks. Can you imagine what it is like to hear five- and six-year- old children cry themselves to sleep until antibiotics gave them relief?

In fairness, we must all be mindful of the thousands of good and decent Canadians—many of them Anglicans and the very backbone of your Church—who put their lives on hold for little pay and hardly any sleep, who went forth to serve the Church, their Lord, and Canadian Indigenous children with kindness, honour, respect, and faith.

Now all they ask for—many from beyond the grave—is a little recognition of some of the good things they did. They ask for nothing more. Senator Beyak was carrying the voices of these forgotten Anglicans to you and to other Canadians when she spoke up in the Senate hearing.

A good deal of evidence exists, in published accounts, correspondence, and conversations that I have had with former IRS workers and students, that my experiences were quite typical. But while some parts of the TRC's Final Report acknowledge those positive and very human experiences, the picture that the *Summary* and *Legacy* volumes of the Report and the media have given to the Canadian public is a partial and skewed version of the IRS reality that many Indigenous children experienced.

When I, as a 21-year-old university student, became a residential supervisor in Stringer Hall in 1966, I could not imagine that many years later, the Anglican Church would express regret and guilt about its management and support of Indian residential schools and hostels. Neither could I imagine that the Anglican employees and supporters of those residential institutions would be vilified by Church leaders for their involvement in a Christian mission that, at the time, seemed so worthwhile and so very necessary.

There are, I think, at least three things that you, Bishop MacDonald, and Archdeacon Thompson, could do to recognize the role that these selfless Christians played in the history of Indian residential schools. First, you could encourage those who worked in the IRS system and those who once were students to talk more about *all* their experiences, not just the negative ones. Second, as Anglicans say their Sunday prayers, and especially when they say prayers for you, Bishop

MacDonald, and the residential school Survivors, you, as leaders of the Church, could remind parishioners to offer up a few prayers for the thousands of committed but forgotten Christians who worked tirelessly, often in dangerous and difficult circumstances, for long hours and with extraordinarily little pay, helping IRS children. Finally, the Anglican Church itself could officially—and bravely—recognize the excellent work that many committed Christians did in Anglican missions that, at the time, seemed so appropriate—even imperative—but is now devalued and vilified by those who refer to everything that happened to Indigenous students in these institutions as 'cultural genocide'..." [25]

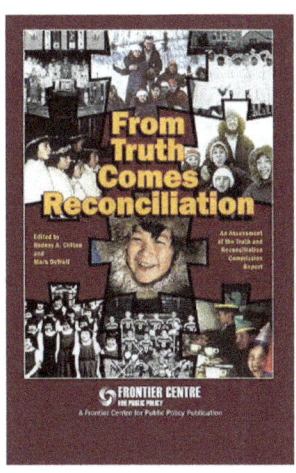

SOURCES

1. "North American Indigenous Warfare and Ritual Violence" by Richard J. Chacon and Rubén G. Mendoza, "Cannibalism, Headhunting and Human Sacrifice in North America: A History Forgotten" by George Feldman, "Archaeological Perspectives on Warfare on the Great Plains" by Andrew Clark, "First Peoples in Canada" by Allan McMillan, "The First Frontier: The Forgotten History of Struggle, Savagery, & Endurance in Early America" by Scott Weidensaul, "Bloody Mohawk: The French and Indian War & American Revolution on New York's Frontier" by Richard Berleth, "Cherokee Mythology: Gods, Myths, Legends and Spiritual Beliefs of the Cherokee Tribe" by Jim Barrow, "Indians of the Yosemite Valley and Vicinity, Their History Customs and Traditions" by Galen Clark, "Prehistoric Lakeheaders: The 90-Century Story of Pre-Contact Thunderbayans" by Alan Wade, "The Four Voyages of Christopher Columbus: Being His Own Log-Book, Letters and Dispatches with Connecting Narratives" by Christopher Columbus, "The Journals of Alexander Mackenzie: Exploring Across Canada in 1789 & 1793" by Alexander Mackenzie, "The History of the Catholic Church in Canada 1659-1895" by Adrian Gabriel Morice. "Converging Worlds Text and Sourcebook" by Louise Breen.
2. Illinois State Museum Website.
3. "The Osteology and Archeology of the Crow Creek Massacre" by P. Willey and E. Emerson.
4. "The Aztecs Constructed this Tower Out of Hundreds of Human Skulls" by Livia Gershon, "A 500-Year-Old Aztec Tower of Human Skulls is Even More Terrifyingly Humongous Than Previously Thought, Archeologists Find" by Sarah Cascone.
5. "Scalp Dance: Indian Warfare on the High Plains, 1865-1879" by Thomas Goodrich.
6. "War before Civilization: The Myth of the Peaceful Savage" by Lawrence Keelay, "Indian Fights and Fighters: The Soldier and the Sioux" by Cyrus Brady, "The First Frontier: The Forgotten History of Struggle, Savagery, & Endurance in Early America"

by Scott Weidensaul, "Captured by the Indians: 15 Firsthand Accounts" by Frederick Drimmer, "Aztec Warfare: Imperial Expansion and Political Control" by Ross Hassig, "Conquests and Cultures: An International History" by Thomas Sowell.
7. "The Popes and Slavery" by Joel S. Panzer.
8. "The Jesuit Relations: Natives and Missionaries in Seventeenth-Century North America" by Allan Greer.
9. "The Indian Act" (1876).
10. "Treaties of Canada with the Indians of Manitoba and the North-West Territories" by Alexander Morris, "Indian Treaties in the United States: An Encyclopedia and Documents Collection" by Donald Fixico, "American Indian Treaties: The History of a Political Anomaly" by Francis Prucha, "Treaties 1 and 2 Between Her Majesty The Queen and the Chippewa and Cree Indians of Manitoba and Country Adjacent with Adhesions" (1871)
11. "Sessional Papers" (1887)
12. "Native American Drinking: Life Styles, Alcohol Use, Drunken Comportment, Problem Drinking, and the Peyote Religion" by Dr. Thomas W. Hill, "Firewater: How Alcohol is Killing My People (and Yours)" by Harold R Johnson, "The League Against King Alcohol" by Professor Thomas J. Lappas, Indian Affairs Annual Report, 1868.
13. "Correspondence Regarding Reports of Destitution and Starvation Among Indians" (1888), "Correspondence, Memoranda, Accounts and Newspaper Clippings Regarding Starvation and Destitution Among the Indians and Eskimos of Labrador" (1883-1906).
14. Sessional Papers from Canadian Parliamentary Historical Resources.
15. "They Came for the Children" by the Truth and Reconciliation Commission of Canada.
16. "Indian Affairs Annual Report," 1920.
17. "Canada's Residential Schools: The History, Part 1, Origins to 1939: The Final Report of the Truth and Reconciliation Commission of Canada, Volume 1" by Truth and Reconciliation Commission of Canada.
18. "Statement of the Governor General of Canada on Indian Policy" (1969).
19. "Thomson Highway Has A surprisingly Positive Take on Residential Schools" by Joshua Ostroff.

20. "Letters to Former Senator Beyek" *https://c2cjournal.ca/2018/04/letters-to-senator-beyak-uncensored/*
21. "School Days: The Residential School Experience" *https://brianholdsworth.ca/images/downloads/school_experience.pdf*
22. "Letter to Sun Columnist" by Jim Bissell *https://www.actforcanada.ca/l/a-reply-to-a-sun-columnist-related-to-the-residential-schools-that-is-leading-to-church-terrorism-by-non-native-people/*
23. "Residential School Column in News/North Draws Criticism From N.W.T. Elders" by Josh Campbell *https://www.cbc.ca/news/canada/north/cece-mccauley-column-1.4490429*
24. "Rescued From the Memory Hole: Some First Nations People Loved Their Residential Schools" LifeSite News Staff *https://www.lifesitenews.com/news/rescued-from-the-memory-hole-some-first-nations-people-loved-their-residential-schools/*
25. "An Open Letter to the Primate of the Anglican Church of Canada" by Rodney A. Clifton *https://hymie.substack.com/p/my-experience-in-indian-residential*

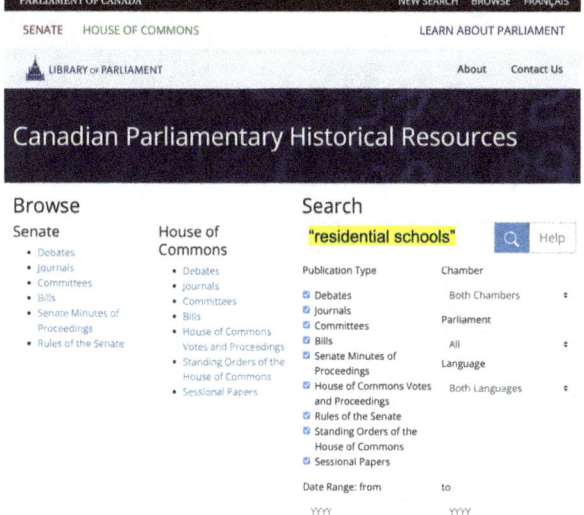

PHOTOGRAPHS

1. The cover image is a photograph of Kamloops Residential School, circa 1930. It's from Archives Deschatelets-NDC, Richelieu and is in the public domain.

2. The archaeological illustrations and photographs on pages 4-7 are from Illinois State Museum: *http://www.museum.state.il.us/RiverWeb/landings/Ambot/prehistory/archives/images/society/thumbnail/ulthm7.htm*

3. The illustration of the scalping on page 8 is from the 1919 edition of 1884 children's book "Indian History for Young Folks" by Francis S. Drake: *https://www.heritage-history.com/index.php?c=read&author=drake&book=indians&story=_front*

4. The photograph on page 24 is of Andrew Paul. It is from the directory of federal heritage: *https://www.pc.gc.ca/apps/dfhd/page_nhs_eng.aspx?id=13334*

5. The photograph on page 8 is of Ahab Spence. It is from an educational website called Inspire: *https://indspire.ca/laureate/ahab-spence-2/*

6. The photograph on page 36 is from Lower Post Residential School from a Catholic education website: *https://www.catholiceducation.org/en/culture/history/the-other-side-of-the-residential-school-question.html*

7. The screenshots of quotations are from various entries in the Canadian Parliamentary Historical Records.

*All photographs are for educational purposes.

UPDATE

2022

I am pleased to learn that, a year after the reported mass grave discovery, the church burnings and the publication of this article in 2021, not a single body has been found. While it is true that many Indigenous children tragically died from illnesses or were victims of abuse, there is no evidence that any were murdered and secretly buried.

It seems that the initial claim was based on soil disturbance found using a technology called "ground penetrating radar." Dr. Sarah Beaulieu found anomalies and seems to have prematurely reported them as "probable burials." A tooth that was "possibly human" was also found. But over the past year, there have been investigations. It turns out that the tooth wasn't human. There are disturbances in the soil because the school has a long history of building things like roads or pipes for irrigation there. Moreover, excavations seem to have been going on at the site for decades. No secret graves have yet been discovered.

For more information on the mistakes and exaggerations that led to the tragic attacks on our churches, I highly recommend the following articles:

SUGGESTIONS FOR FURTHER READING

2022

"One Year Later Still No Evidence of Unmarked Graves"
 - Retired Judge, Brian Giesbrecht

"In Kamloops, Not One Body Has Been Found"
 - Professor Jacques Rouillard

"The False Narrative of Residential School Burials"
 - Professor Tom Flanagan

"From Truth Comes Reconciliation: Assessing the Truth and Reconciliation Commission Report"
 - Dr. Rodney A. Clifton, Mark Dewolf

"Billy Remembers: Analyzing the Tk'emlúps te Secwépemc/Kamloops Indian Residential School Moral Panic."
 - Dr. Frances Widdowson

"Where are the Children Buried?
 - Dr. Scott Hamilton

SUGGESTIONS FOR FURTHER READING 75

"A Narrative Reversal Like No Other"
  - James Pew

"Len Marchand's Indian Residential School Experience"
  - James C. McCrae

"Digging for the Truth About Canada's Residential Schools Graves"
  - Hymie Rubenstein

"The Year of the Graves: How the Worlds Media Got it Wrong on Residential School Graves"
  - National Post

"No Evidence of Unmarked Graves Related to Shubenacadie Residential School: Researchers Say Evidence of Unmarked Graves was Found During Search, But They Pre-Date School"
  - CBC

"The Indigenous Mass Grave That Wasn't"
  - The Spectator

"No Unmarked Graves Found at Nova Scotia Residential School"
  - National Post

"Why an Oji-Cree Community is Trying to Rebuild its Catholic Church"
  - CBC

ABOUT THE AUTHOR

Drew Eldridge is a tutor from Winnipeg, Manitoba. He has a Bachelor of Arts Degree, majoring in English from the University of Winnipeg, specializing in Young People's Texts and Cultures.